Sally McManus is the tenth elected Australian Council of Trade Unions Secretary in the organisation's 90-year history and the first woman to hold the position. She was previously the NSW and ACT Secretary of the Australian Services Union and ACTU Campaigns Director.

Writers in the *On Series*

Sally McManus
On Fairness

Every attempt has been made to locate the copyright holders for material quoted in this book. Any person or organisation that may have been overlooked or misattributed may contact the publisher.

hachette
AUSTRALIA

Published in Australia and New Zealand in 2020
by Hachette Australia
(an imprint of Hachette Australia Pty Limited)
Level 17, 207 Kent Street, Sydney NSW 2000
www.hachette.com.au

First published in 2019 by Melbourne University Publishing

10 9 8 7 6 5 4 3 2 1

A catalogue record for this book is available from the National Library of Australia

ISBN: 978 0 7336 4431 3

Original cover concept by Nada Backovic Design
Text design and typesetting by Alice Graphics
Author photograph by Nikki Toole
Printed and bound in Australia by McPherson's Printing Group

Transcript from *7.30*, ABC Television, 15 March 2017

Posted at 7.59pm

LEIGH SALES: … Will the ACTU consider distancing itself from the CFMEU, which has faced 118 separate legal proceedings where it's been found to have either broken the law or acted in contempt of court?

SALLY MCMANUS: There's no way we will be doing that. I'll tell you this: the CFMEU, when they have been fined, they have been fined for taking industrial action—

LEIGH SALES: —Illegal industrial action?

SALLY MCMANUS: It might be illegal industrial action—according to our current laws … and our current laws are wrong. It shouldn't be so hard for workers in our country to be able to take industrial action when they need to. Quite often these workers have stopped work because a worker has been killed on a building site. And—know this—that union gets fined more than the companies that actually kill workers …

LEIGH SALES: Yet nonetheless, we live in a country where there are laws that are established by a parliament that all citizens are expected to abide by. So, regardless of whether you agree or disagree with those laws, you said that you believe in the rule of law?

SALLY MCMANUS: Yeah, I believe in the rule of law where the law is fair, when the law is right. But when it's unjust, I don't think there's a problem with breaking it.

Fronting up to *7.30* is pretty much a rite of passage for a new ACTU Secretary.

You know the various media outlets will run a whole lot of stories. They'll mainly be 'profile' pieces—which I hate. Their relentless focus is to discern a single 'eureka' moment to explain what made you who you are, as the sum of your personal history and feelings— inevitably minimising what has actually shaped you, which, for an ACTU Secretary, is the collective history of, and activity within, the organised movement of working people. So many people just don't get this.

But appearing on *7.30* is another matter entirely. Becoming ACTU Secretary makes you the representative of 1.8 million people, and you have to stand and deliver for every member. It's a bit like being an opening batsperson in their first test match, and—in terms of fast bowlers—presenter Leigh Sales is Glenn McGrath in his prime. You know there will be bouncers coming right at your head. You can duck, you can try to block, or you can get on the front foot … but you have less than a second to make up your mind how you will respond.

My Leigh Sales encounter occurred less than four hours after I became ACTU Secretary. That morning, the leadership of all Australia's unions had met in Melbourne to decide the formal appointment. I waited, the meeting announced its decision, then I stood to take the Secretary's seat, next to the President, Ged Kearney. There was excitement; for the first time in its 90-year history, the ACTU had a woman Secretary, as well as a woman president—positions that, twenty years ago, were exclusively held by men. The formalities were concluded, photos were taken, and I was whisked away to the ABC studio, and thrust into a makeup chair.

I've never been one for wearing makeup, and, at forty-five years of age, was confronted both with the immediate need to prepare for Sales' impending bouncers, and my disempowering lack of capacity to issue any clear preferences to the ABC makeup staff. I felt growing horror when my face as I knew it disappeared under the makeup-mirror lights. I don't mind pressure—I rather like it—but

the reflection of a pancaked face I did not rec-
ognise was truly disconcerting.

The Melbourne ABC studio was like
something from a 1970s sci-fi set; a small,
dark box of a room, with bits of gaffer tape
all over the place, and the crew behind a glass
wall. Someone put a flesh-coloured screw
that looked like a medical instrument into my
ear. My swivel chair was not comfortable. I
asked, 'Where's Leigh Sales?'

'Oh, she's in Sydney.'

'How will I talk to her?'

A technician pointed at the other side of
the room, to a camera with a screen: 'She'll
appear there.' I was left alone with the dead
lens looking at me, unblinking and silent.

Then into my earpiece came a voice: 'Sally,
can you hear me? We'll start in five minutes.'

Five minutes is a long time to sit in a silent black box, waiting for a fast bowler you can't see.

'Four minutes.'

The camera remained silent.

'Three minutes … Two minutes …'

God.

'One minute …'

Jesus.

'Thirty seconds.'

Like a hologram, Leigh Sales appeared in the camera, distant and small. Makeup artists hovered around her, and I wondered if she could even see me, until the precise moment she said, 'All right, Sally—let's go.' Then, it all sprang suddenly to life—the camera in front of me, Leigh, and my new reality as ACTU Secretary.

Lots of people have asked me if I 'planned' what happened in the interview … as if anyone can plan something like that. I hadn't planned my answers, just as I hadn't planned my makeup.

The only thing I did ever plan was to be on the front foot.

I love the union movement. When I was a student at Carlingford High School in the late 1980s, my teachers took strike action against unjust education cuts by the New South Wales Liberal government. With my friends, I caught the train into the city to show support, joining a mass gathering in Sydney's Domain.

We were protesting bigger class sizes, and losing teachers in the middle of our HSC year, at the end of a decade when lots of communities across the English-speaking West had been experiencing similar cuts to public sector jobs. It was part of a new right-wing economic agenda that insisted things like education, or the supply of water, or transport, health and electricity generation, could be done more efficiently by the private sector, with more outsourcing, and fewer permanent jobs. It was, of course, the era of Margaret Thatcher in the UK, and Ronald Reagan in the United States. I had grown up listening to the protest songs of punk bands from overseas, but now this ideology—and the protests that accompanied them—had hit my city and my school.

There'd been protest movements concerned with similar issues springing up in Victoria; earlier than that, South Australia;

and, earlier still, in New Zealand. The consistent tactic of the organised right was to take on the industries with the strongest unions, banking on early victories to demoralise the broader union movement, just as Nick Greiner's newly elected Liberal government picked a fight with the New South Wales Teachers Federation.

But the Teachers Federation fought back. Teachers, parents, students and communities are rarely united, but the federation mobilised them all to defend public schools from the ideology of funding cuts and mass layoffs; these were some of the largest union protests Sydney had ever seen. And I was there—in the city heart that kids from my suburb visited rarely, standing with tens of thousands of people.

The spectacle of that gathering, the might of its unified purpose, the feeling of solidarity and strength, resonated with me in a way that has shaped my beliefs and my actions ever since. Union power is this simple act of solidarity—of people realising what we have in common, and deciding both to stick together and to act.

I'm proud of today's unions, and of the history that has brought us to this point; a history that unionists are keen to share with each new generation. When I started as a trainee union organiser with the Australian Services Union, five years after that teachers strike, the ACTU provided us with 'mentors' or 'elders' as part of our education: mine were Tom McDonald, a former Secretary of the Building Workers' Industrial Union, and

Tas Bull, former Secretary of the Maritime Union. The two men had led huge, successful campaigns during their careers, winning for all Australians really big things such as the provision of superannuation, and workers compensation for workplace injury. Now retired, they shared with us the stories of how these battles were won and the sacrifices involved in winning. What the organised movement of working people has endured to deliver the living standards all Australians now enjoy were lessons us young organisers treasured.

None of it was easily won. Nothing. Basic, reasonable demands, like a 38-hour working week, and even Medicare, were won or defended by union members campaigning, protesting and mobilising, at great personal risk and cost to themselves. Our movement's most important achievements were won by breaking unjust laws, because it has nearly always been illegal to take strike action.

From the origins of modern trade unions during the Industrial Revolution, to the Australia of today, workers have always confronted a threat of state-sanctioned punishment when they've decided to take action in their own industrial interest. Violence, the police, mercenaries and the military have been used across time and across the world to bust strikes, persecute union leaders and suppress worker protests. Early British trade unionists used to swear oaths of allegiance to their cause on pictures of skeletons, knowing the price of forming an illegal 'combination'—a union—could be death. In Canberra, a monument commemorates the

Tolpuddle Martyrs, a group of Dorset agricultural labourers who, in the 1830s, were punished with transportation to the brutal penal colony of Australia when their attempts to form a union were discovered. The pattern is consistent in different cultures, and across continents: in 1903, the American state of Colorado imposed martial law in order to put down strikes by gold and silver miners. In Australia, in 1929, police similarly opened fire on a protest march of locked-out coalminers in the New South Wales town of Rothbury, killing one man and injuring forty-five others.

These are not isolated incidents. Rather, they're examples of ongoing attempts to demoralise and demobilise working people. The tactics, of course, are not limited to state violence. Unknown actors were behind the assassination of trade union leader Shankar Guha Niyogi in India in 1991; the public execution of a Cambodian trade union leader, Chea Vichea in 2004; and even the lethal bombing—a crime that's still unsolved—of the Trades Hall in Wellington, New Zealand, in 1984, which caused the death of caretaker Ernie Abbott. Today, trade union leaders are jailed and prosecuted in countries like Iran and South Korea; in Guatemala, as of 2017, eighty-seven union leaders have been murdered since 2004. Over the years, anti-union, strike-breaking tactics have also included exorbitant fines, jail sentences, raids, mass sackings, lengthy litigations, social ostracism, propaganda campaigns, organised harassment and bullying, as well as vilification in the media, to punish workers taking action in the interests of industrial fairness for themselves, and in the interests of a fairer society. Locally, in 2018, a blackmail case against Victorian Construction Forestry Maritime Mining and Energy Union leaders John Setka and Shaun Reardon was thrown out of court, but only after two years of the men's phones being tapped, and of the police following them in public, arrests in front of their children, and the conservative media and the Liberal Party portraying them as criminal thugs. The case was abandoned when key prosecution witnesses from a multinational concreting company who were supposedly subject to the blackmailing were found to be at risk of perjuring themselves if they gave evidence, while other witnesses categorically denied the version of events the prosecution had tried to paint.

Something I'm most proud of as an Australian unionist are those times that working people have fought for justice far beyond their own workplace or industry. In the years leading up to World War II, Australian unions refused to load ships with pig-iron bound for Japan, knowing that the cargo was destined for the manufacture of armaments used in the Japanese militarisation and expansionism that caused the war in the Pacific.

Australian unions also refused to unload ships, and participated in a wider boycott of goods, from South Africa when Nelson Mandela was in jail; by doing so, they joined the international movement that helped bring down apartheid. One of the first places

Nelson Mandela visited when he was freed from jail and again allowed to travel was Australia, and he thanked the Australian trade union movement, specifically the ACTU, for its campaigns of solidarity.

In Sydney, construction unions refused to bulldoze heritage buildings, wreck low-income housing or tear up bushland in what became known as the 'green bans' movement of the 1970s. The Secretary of the New South Wales Builders Labourers' Federation, Jack Mundey, was arrested for his part in the protests in 1973.

All these powerful acts of solidarity involved challenging or breaking unjust laws. Even though they are celebrated now, at the time they were not popular, and unions and their leaders were the targets of relentless attacks from conservative media. Yet, all Australians have had the benefits from the stand these workers and the unions took. They variously risked violence, jail, fines and unemployment to fight to realise greater principles.

In most developed countries, a working person's right to withdraw their labour in protest is accepted as an essential part of democracy. Many nations even guarantee it in their constitutions, so that no government may undermine it. The International Labour Organization agrees; the right to strike is a human right.

Yet, the Australia of today finds itself with some of the most restrictive anti-strike laws in the developed world. The right to strike in this country was severely curtailed during the years of the John Howard Coalition government, culminating in the draconian WorkChoices legislation. Although the Fair Work Act replaced WorkChoices, our framework of industrial fairness has not recovered.

If a group of Australian working people decided to stop work today to protest the actions of their employer, their punishment for doing so could be substantial. They'd face the loss of a minimum of four hours' pay—even for a 10-minute stoppage—as well as fines of up to $12,600 each. In addition, their union would face fines of up to $35,000 because of the action. There are multiple other potential penalties, and employers can sue for damages.

Yes, in our country, exercising the human right to withdraw your labour can cost you your financial security; maybe even your house. There is nothing fair about this.

It's little wonder that strike actions—and pay rises—are at record lows.

How we got to this point can be explained by what happened to me in that black box at the ABC studio, because the same tactic is tried the world over, from television interviews to courtrooms, to parliamentary proceedings. When union leaders are asked whether we support the 'rule of law', we're being challenged to abandon and condemn our own history, as well as the union members who stand up for themselves and go on strike, lest we risk our own reputations as upstanding citizens. The implicit threat is that should we associate ourselves with 'law breaking'—even if the laws in question are unjust—we'll position both ourselves and the institutions we represent as suspect:

potentially criminal, and unworthy of the public's high regard.

We're supposed to be timid in the face of this disapproval. But timidity comes at a cost far greater than a bit of external consternation. Disavowing the right to strike weakens every worker's rightful claim to it. Again, these questions implicitly demand we renounce our support for the generations of union members who fought and suffered to give us all the living standards we have today.

And there's just no way I'll be doing that.

Respect for the rule of law is about belief in the capacity of that law to dispense justice, fairness and equality for all. But laws aren't passed by principles—they're passed by governments, and governments can be unjust and unfair. Our anti-strike laws are one of many manifestations of this fact. Apartheid in South Africa, the dominion of the British Raj over India, and race segregation in the United States of America, were entirely 'legal' regimes, and governed by laws that restricted the most basic democratic rights and freedoms. It's no coincidence that Nelson Mandela, Mahatma Gandhi and Martin Luther King Jr were all active trade unionists. Since our first members swore oaths on those old pictures of skeletons, our movement has known that breaking laws and risking punishment is sometimes necessary, because it is the only moral path to fairness.

I'd suggest that Australians who disagree consider this argument the next time they visit a hospital. The Australian union movement called an 'illegal' general strike in 1976, when

Prime Minister Malcolm Fraser's government was trying to destroy our embryonic universal healthcare system. That strike brought the country to a standstill. Fraser backed down, and what became Medicare remains. The same people who disagree may also want to reflect on this the next time they enjoy a leisurely weekend, or are saved from an accident by workplace safety standards, or knock off work after an eight-hour shift. Union members won all these conditions in campaigns that were deemed 'illegal' industrial action at the time. These union members built the living standards we all enjoy. They should be celebrated and thanked for their bravery and sacrifices, not condemned and renounced.

Yeah, I believe in the rule of law where the law is fair, when the law is right. But when it's unjust, I don't think there's a problem with breaking it.

At the time, I had no idea that my answer would provoke any great reaction. However, I do remember the ACTU media officer was looking a bit pale when I emerged from the black box.

But the interview was over, and I was ending my first day as ACTU Secretary, feeling a similar euphoria to that when you leave a dentist without new fillings and with no need to come back for a year. To my mind, I'd faced some Leigh Sales bouncers, having managed to dispatch a few. My immediate concern was getting the makeup off.

Anyone who wants to see the deep cultural anger Australians have towards unfairness need only look at the abuse heaped upon sporting umpires. Across our country, 'football' can mean many different codes, whether AFL, league, rugby or soccer, and people can be devoted to cricket, basketball, tennis or anything else, but the attitude to the umpire is universal. Even the deep hatred fans cultivate towards a rival team or player is nothing compared with what is unleashed at any suggestion of unfairness by the umpire. If Australians at a sporting match suspect that the game is rigged, that there is no 'level playing field' or that the independent umpire is not independent, rage erupts. This kind of response may not be uniquely Australian, but the insults Australians level certainly are. If you're unfamiliar with the idiom we employ and like some colour, I suggest googling 'Australians insult referee'. No wonder so many sports have needed a video referee.

This commitment to fairness is deeply ingrained across many facets of our culture, and is a distinctive quality in comparison with other English-speaking Western countries. Donald Horne made the point in his book *The Lucky Country*, more than fifty years ago, that 'life in Australia is more equal and less competitive than in America', and we eschew defaulting to the privileges of a hereditary class system that remains a feature of other countries. There are few Australians who wouldn't define the culture's adherence to 'the fair go' as our most important national belief.

Various dictionaries define the term as meaning 'an even-handed, reasonable chance or equitable opportunity to attempt something'. So ingrained as an Australian virtue is the concept of both giving and receiving a 'fair go' that both sides of politics cite it to justify policy decisions as much as do amateur sporting commentators when they're yelling at the ref. The Australian National Dictionary Centre describes the term as both 'iconic and resonant' for our history and our people.

The centre's research has also revealed it has a specific trade union origin. The first recorded usage of the term is on page five of the *Brisbane Courier*, 25 March 1891, in the context of the brutal Shearers' Strike that took place that year. The paper was reporting a campaign of forced and violent dispersal by police of the unionists gathered in camps around Queensland's Rockhampton. Amid raids and arrests, 'a report was spread industriously', recorded the paper, that a special train was arriving in Clermont, bearing a cargo of non-union labour. Unionists arrived at the train station to protest—only to discover that the train contained their own imprisoned comrades, and it was a trap.

The *Courier* recounts that, having cleared the station, police inspectors—backed by twenty-five members of the Artillery, and in the company of a Mr Ranking from the shearers' employers, the Pastoralists' Executive—then announced they had warrants for the arrest of two union leaders who were present, men by the names of Taylor and Stewart. What then followed is familiar:

'What for?' asked both men with a laugh.

'For conspiracy,' was the reply, and in a twinkling the handcuffs were out.

Both men turned pale, but struggled, calling out, 'Read the warrants to us first.' Inspector Ahern said, 'You can hear them later,' and the police seized the prisoners.

Both appealed to Mr Ranking, crying out, 'Do you call this a fair go, Mr Ranking?' Taylor's resistance was met with force, and he became quiet, and asked to be allowed to give certain papers to a friend in the crowd.

'Oh, no,' said Inspector Ahern, 'We may want them.'

The papers and other articles were then taken from his pockets and placed in a handkerchief, and the search of Stewart was proceeded with.

As a demand for justice amid injustice, and for recognition of rights at the very scene of their deprivation, the 'fair go' speaks not only to the moment of its utterance, in 1891 or at some other time. According to the centre, it speaks more broadly of, and to, a historical trajectory from 'unionised labour, workers' rights and Labor governments', to an Australia that's 'an egalitarian society—a "workers' paradise"'. The 'fair go' is a vision of Australian potential, coming from the same yearning of Banjo Paterson's narrator in 'Clancy of the Overflow', who's stirred from 'the round eternal of the cashbook and the journal' to imagine an Australia beyond his workplace, as somewhere work can, indeed, entail instead a 'vision splendid of the sunlit plains extended, and at night the wond'rous glory of the everlasting stars'. Paterson's most famous work, 'Waltzing Matilda'—in which a man who steals a sheep commits suicide rather than be punished by an unjust law for the crime of feeding himself—is an allegory for the Shearers' Strike mentioned above.

These specific cultural traditions of the 'fair go' imagined fairness in a way that was not universally applied. The 'fair go' of the last century ignored the bitter battles that women had to fight for legal equality in the community and the workforce, and it was wilfully, dangerously blind to the dispossession of Aboriginal and Torres Strait Islanders, and the brutal reality of the racism and exploitation on which modern Australia was built. Wider social inequalities and discriminations manifest in the workplace too. But campaigns for empathy and solidarity—in which unions played their part—have expanded the 'fair go' into an ideal whose power has grown as it has extended its reach, evolving into something that has spurred so much of our history, our art and literature, our cultural habits and national character, it's unsurprising that the opponents of fairness are somewhat desperate to steal the language of the 'fair go' to make their own.

It's why people like the current Prime Minister, Scott Morrison, drop corrupting catchphrases like 'a *fair go* for those who have a go' into the national conversation, to impose their own distinction between those Australians they have decided are deserving, and others who are, somehow, undeserving of opportunity. The fairness these people suggest is always conditional, a pledge to provide chances only to those who 'make a contribution, not seek one', to reward only those who meet their criteria for being 'lifters', as opposed to the 'leaners', who get nothing.

Their mugging of 'fairness' is, of course, a con—and one that can only work for as long as they continue to convince people that their lack of opportunity is either their own fault, or something that can be blamed on whichever local outsiders, or minorities, are most easily portrayed as villainous interlopers.

But when it's obvious that material conditions have become so unbalanced in favour of one group over another that you can work hard, obey all the rules and not get ahead; when people start talking, and realise that what many were promised, few have received;

when a factory's whole workforce is fired from their jobs, only to have the same work offered to them recontracted as 'sub-contracting' or 'labour hire', at a much lower rate; when a stroke of a pen in a distant court cuts a weekend worker's pay; when you're told that opportunity's a level playing field, but you can see you're really standing on a slope, at the bottom of a hill ... that's when the falsity becomes transparent, and the scapegoating wears thin.

That's precisely when Australians start howling at the ref.

They're howling now.

In the Australia we live in today, it has not escaped notice that remuneration for company bosses continues to ascend to stratospheric levels, while the people who work at the companies these people run struggle to get a pay rise.

The *Sydney Morning Herald* recently reported that the chief executive officers of Australia's 100 richest companies enjoyed a median salary rise of 12.4 per cent over the course of 2017. The ABC reported that CEOs from the next hundred richest companies had enjoyed a pay rise of more than 22.1 per cent in the same period, with the CEOs of all publicly listed companies reaping a pay rise of 9.3 per cent on average. 'Persistent and increasing bonus payments'—which are on top of salaries, and themselves rose 18 per cent in that year—were cited as the reason that company bosses' pay had reached its highest level in seventeen years. At the same time, wage growth for the average Australian worker has flatlined; while the CEOs were enjoying their fortunes, the Wage Price Index for everyone else grew a mere 2.1 per cent, and struggled to keep pace with inflation. The boss of Domino's Pizza, Don Meij, was the highest-paid chief executive in Australia in 2017. He alone was paid $36.84 million. This is 435 times the average full-time wage.

Working people and their families have become aware of this discrepancy, just as they're aware that as bonus season rolls around, and more record profits are announced, the job security of working Australians continues to slide. The number of Australians in 'casual' work, as defined by the Australian Bureau of Statistics, has nearly doubled since the 1980s, from 13 per cent of workers to more than 25 per cent now. But even more insidious has been the growth in 'non-standard workers', whose employment contracts classify them as 'owner-managers'. They work the same jobs but sub-contractors, enjoy none of the conditions—like leave entitlements or protection from unfair dismissal—that the law demands for people contracted as employees. This employment model has been forced on workers ranging from fruit-pickers, to cleaners, to electricians and machinists, to academics, journalists, and just about everyone working in the gig economy, any of whom can find themselves dismissed at any time. This kind of contracting has ballooned in Australia—some of our largest companies have used it to outsource parts of their existing workforce back to these same workers, with stripped conditions, and at reduced cost to the employers. An International Organisation for Economic Cooperation and Development report ranked Australia third in the world for non-standard forms of work. Added up, the self-employed, the part-time workers, casual workers and those on fixed-term contracts are now 44 per cent of the Australian workforce. In comparison, the OECD average is a third of the national workplace. In addition, Jim Stanford from the Centre for Future Work suggests less than half of employed Australians now hold a 'standard' job: that is, a permanent, full-time paid job with leave entitlements.

When the exhausted teenage 'owner-manager', delivering pizzas all night for less money an hour than one pizza costs, loses shifts for no reason—or never gets called in to work again—there is no compensation. Yet, in 2015, the year that annual wage growth among the broader populace dropped to its lowest level on record, corporate executives hit a record of their own—for retirement payouts. The *Australian Financial Review* reported that $30 million had been paid in 'golden handshakes' to retiring executives in that single year. One of them, Hamish Tyrwhitt, the CEO of infrastructure company CIMIC (formerly Leighton), took home $13.59 million—even after the new owners of the company had fired him.

The *AFR* had the good grace to mention that corporate pay had exceeded fifty times the average Australian salary—but by 2017, the gap had *increased*. In only two years, the ABC was reporting that CEOs were earning a whopping 78 times as much, with CEO pay growing at 46 per cent year on year against the average income.

Inequality is visible to Australians. It's my greatest privilege as ACTU Secretary to spend most of my time in conversations with working people, listening to the insights and experiences of union members in every conceivable occupation. Road workers, nurses, boilermakers, teachers, meteorologists, musicians and truck drivers ... I criss-cross the country, from Mount Isa to Hobart, Penrith to Fremantle, meeting them. There are many things that unite members, but that deep, shared hatred of what is unfair is always palpable. Union members will stand together, whether it's against a bullying local manager, or an entire wages system that profits only the very few, but there's one issue that always receives unanimous and overwhelming support from the people I meet—that everyone needs to pay their fair share of tax.

Australia's unionists may not all know the complexities of how tax avoidance operates, and they may not be across the ins and outs of each tax-minimising loophole and rort, but the reluctance of Australia's rich to make taxation contributions that are in any way proportional to their wealth is as well known as it is enraging. When I explain to meetings of our members that there are sixty-two Australians who each earned $1 million last year and paid not one cent in tax—not even the Medicare levy—it is *pitchfork time*.

Tax minimisation is not merely the preserve of rich individuals. Last year, as reported in *The Guardian*, 732 of Australia's biggest companies—those very companies rewarding their executives with gargantuan bonuses—did not pay one cent of tax. These businesses relied on roads, airports, water, public health systems, police, fire protection and other taxpayer-funded infrastructure, for their operations to be viable and profitable. And that profit, returned to shareholders, was subsidised by shop assistants, hospitality workers, council employees, early childhood educators, plasterers, hospital orderlies, and everyone else who doesn't have the funds—or the lack of ethics—to hire specialist tax minimisation lawyers, year after year … or the power to persuade the government to legislate further tax advantages for them.

In 2016, the first-term Liberal–National Party Coalition, then led by Malcolm Turnbull, went to a federal election, promising the Australian people 'Jobs and Growth'. It won with the slenderest of majorities: only one seat. It then announced its 'jobs plan' to the electorate. In the tradition of the 'trickle-down' economics that has defined the Liberal–National Party world view since Malcolm Fraser became Prime Minister in 1975, it planned tax cuts of unprecedented size for Australia's richest businesses. The idea was that the sudden cash windfall to a company budget would inspire said company to spend money on projects that might employ people.

Policy devised on this basis is how Australia strayed so far from its 'vision splendid' of the fair go, to the record inequality of the present.

The government's thinking goes by many names, depending on when and where it's dominated political debate: free market ideology, economic rationalism, Reaganomics, Thatcherism, the Chicago School, market economics (when it's friendly), neoliberalism (when it's not). Whatever you call it, it remains a form of structured economic unfairness, and it's been political orthodoxy around the world since the 1970s. It was the effects of the New South Wales government trialling neoliberal frameworks for state education that led me to my first union protest in the 1980s.

In the post-World War II period, the Western democracies' governments had economic policies that were more about building institutions and infrastructure, regulating civic behaviour, maintaining full employment levels and providing quality public services, than they were about letting business do whatever it wanted.

But, internationally, 'free market' think-tanks—like our Institute of Public Affairs—campaigned to influence political parties, treasuries, business groups, economists, journalists and academics to believe that a deregulated 'market' of businesses and corporate activity was the best economic means to assign resources to people. They offered powerful groups and individuals the convenient gospel that if you hand wealth to the rich, it will somehow 'trickle down' to the rest of us.

Members of the modern Liberal Party are ideologues of these beliefs. 'If you give businesses the incentive to invest more … they will employ more', Mr Turnbull told reporters when he was spruiking tax cuts in 2018. 'It's always worked in the past. It's pretty basic. It's Economics 101, really … so that's why we're pressing on with our enterprise tax program, because we know that it will result in more investment and more jobs.'

Turnbull and friends should maybe have stuck around for more subjects than 'Economics 101', because what he claimed 'always worked in the past' has never, actually, worked in the past. And in this specific context, the words 'We're not in Kansas anymore' take on an incredibly sad—and relevant—new meaning.

In 2017, *The Washington Post* printed a depressing story. Five years earlier, the state of Kansas was used as a laboratory for one of the world's most radical exercises in trickle-down economics. The Governor, Republican Sam Brownback, announced the state government would slash Kansas' already low tax rates even further, remove income tax for most owner-operated businesses, and shred government services.

Brownback called it 'a shot of adrenaline into the heart of the Kansas economy'. *The Post* instead described it as 'a shot of poison'.

The trickle-down promise of 'more investment and more jobs' did not materialise. Instead, the state deficit shot up to a billion dollars. Cuts to services devastated communities, public service lay-offs entrenched unemployment, and infrastructure started to fray. Meanwhile, higher-taxing neighbouring states enjoyed better growth levels, because— as it turns out—people prefer to live, work and run businesses in places where schools stay open, the water is clean and the roads are not falling apart.

Finally, Brownback's Republican comrades came to their senses and reinstated enough taxes that the state could once again function. But the shortfall in funding has had effects so dire that as recently as April 2018, Kansas schools were still threatened with closure for failing to meet educational standards guaranteed by the United States Constitution. It will take years for all the damage done to be repaired.

As an experiment, it had its benefits—if not for the people of Kansas. It proved to the rest of us, conclusively, these policies *do not work*. Brownback didn't get the implementation wrong, or forget some key part of the theory. He obeyed the orthodoxy, and these policies took Kansas to neoliberalism's inevitable conclusion very quickly.

'Before Kansas,' wrote the *Post*, trickledown advocates 'could at least argue that the program had only been attempted partially and piecemeal, never in full and unadulterated form. After Kansas, that excuse is gone.'

Labor's Paul Keating is the Australian Prime Minister who, in the 1980s, led the most radical remaking of the Australian economy into a neoliberal framework. The government he led moderated the Brownback version of neoliberalism, by retaining investment in expansive social programs, infrastructure and services, and worked with unions to extend and deliver positive initiatives like Medicare and compulsory superannuation. At the

same time, it privatised formerly government-owned assets like the Commonwealth
Bank and Qantas. Keating is remembered
as a 'staunch defender of open markets' by
publications like *The Age*, but he's watched
what neoliberalism's wreaked in the last
thirty years, and come to question its core
assumptions. 'We have a comatose world
economy held together by debt and central
bank money,' he said in March 2017. 'Liberal
economics has run into a dead end and has
had no answer to the contemporary malaise.'

All of this—from Kansas to Keating—was
a matter of public record long before January
2018, when then Treasurer Scott Morrison
fronted the nation and claimed Australia
should 'look to the US' to see how well cor-
porate-tax-cut policies were working.

I was travelling Australia, meeting union members, when the Coalition government—with a lot of handy support from big business—was pushing its proposed tax cuts the hardest. Where I went, workers weren't offering analyses of the role of 'central bank money' in the running of the world economy, but that didn't make their criticisms of the plan to cut corporate tax any less valid. People were asking:

But if they don't pay even their fair share of tax now, why should we let them get away with paying even less?

And:

If they will supposedly give us pay rises when they pay less tax, why aren't any of the companies who pay no tax now already giving pay rises?

They were questions the government deflected, waving to the example of massive corporate tax cuts the US President, Donald Trump, had just introduced that reduced the rate from 35 per cent to 21 per cent across America—again, despite the clear and present example of what had happened in Kansas. As recently as August 2018, the Finance Minister, Mathias Cormann, was still insisting that: 'The evidence on the ground is very clear. The Trump tax cuts have led to stronger investment, stronger growth, lower unemployment rate and higher wages.' But *The Conversation* fact-checked the claim, and discovered that the small gains made in these areas of the US economy weren't caused by the tax cuts, as much as conforming to a pattern of growth that began in 2016, when the nation started to recover properly from the Global Financial Crisis.

Economist and Nobel Laureate Paul Krugman, in *The New York Times* in November 2018, was more blunt: 'A vast majority of businesses say either that the tax law has had no effect on their investment plans, or that they are planning only a modest increase,' he wrote, identifying that the greatest beneficiary of the cuts to date had been shareholders receiving higher returns. It was a fact that inconveniently tallied with the contents of a secret Business Council of Australia (BCA) survey that had been leaked earlier in 2018. The *Australian Financial Review* reported that more than 80 per cent of businesses that responded to the survey planned to return the windfall in dividends to their shareholders or increase capital expenditure, but not to raise wages or create new jobs.

Fortunately, our government lost the vote to pass its own corporate tax cuts, when the other parties and independents joined with the ALP and the Greens in the Senate after they got the message from the electorate that people were not believing the trickle-down promises. When something's intent does not look fair, only a fool could believe its output will be anything like fair. While there are a few fools in Australia, fortunately they are not a majority.

But neither the campaign for corporate tax cuts nor the ideology of neoliberalism that's behind them has been dissipated by the lost Senate vote. Immediately, the BCA was back on the corporate tax cut campaign trail, claiming it was both 'bitterly disappointing' and a 'colossal mistake' that the government had been forced to abandon policies that demonstrably do not work. They then demanded the government find some means of compensating the corporate sector for the loss. And the BCA's spokesperson went on to argue for restricting even further the right of workers to access union representatives at their workplaces, so as to reduce even more the conditions around which employees can negotiate, and to maintain a system that suits them and their bonuses just fine, while wages flatline and job security crumbles.

Rapid growth in wealth inequality results in the inevitable isolation of a very small, very rich, very privileged section of the community from the material experiences of everyone else. And when this out-of-touch minority group is enfranchised to make the decisions on behalf of people they don't know, can't see, have no wish to understand, and think of entirely in dehumanised, transactional, abstract terms, the results for the rest of us are devastating.

Neoliberalism is not just about tax cuts. It relies on a suite of mechanisms to manifest its 'free market' of optimum conditions for business.

Privatisation of government-owned enterprises is crucial to the project. One of the appealing features of tax cuts for neoliberal governments is that reduced revenue provides them with an excuse to sell state assets to meet the sudden budget shortfalls. The sale of state assets creates more lucrative business opportunities for the corporations that can afford to buy such things as power stations, water treatment plants, telecommunications providers, government banks and airlines. It's something of a windfall for a business to acquire an asset that will always deliver a return so long as citizens still need things like water or power supplied to their homes, a bus to catch from one place to another, or a telephone connection. And—unlike a state-owned asset—a private corporation never has to adjust its services due to democratic prompting from the electorate. Why do power prices keep going up across Australia? Because most of the power supply is now owned and operated by private corporations. They're free to price gouge on the supply of an essential service, because they can't be voted out of office.

But privatisation has another important function in the neoliberal world view, and that's to assist wage suppression.

If you're a private company, you've got one overriding obligation, and it's not to your workers, to your country or your community—it's to make a profit, in order to return it in dividends to your shareholders. That's it. And the means to increase that rate of return to its greatest possible margin is cutting the cost of your operation. You do this by increasing your productivity, expanding your market, raising prices on your offered commodities, and by reducing the wages and conditions of the people who work for you. Unionisation, of course, obstructs the extent to which employers are able to squeeze working people in their profit calculations, levelling the playing field between the single, powerful employer and the unified might of an organised workforce.

Across the world, public sector workers typically have higher rates of unionisation than does the private sector. The combination of centralised workplaces, more secure positions, accountability mechanisms applying to government employers, and a correlation between union values and those of the public service, traditionally predisposes the ability of workers to organise, allowing them to assert standards of pay and conditions through collective bargaining.

In economies where jobs in a strong public sector are available, private employers have to compete for workers by offering comparable pay and conditions. The effects of this situation are heightened when a government uses direct public service employment to meet the terms of a full employment policy, because the workers aren't so afraid of unemployment they will bargain their workplace pay and conditions down just to avoid what happens when you're on Newstart.

For the thirty years from the World War II John Curtin Labor government, to the end of the Gough Whitlam Labor one in the 1970s, Australia had such a policy. Curtin's 1945 *White Paper on Full Employment* outlined a program to create jobs in nation-building infrastructure projects, as well as a mass expansion of social services. His government had observed that while Australian unemployment levels did not drop below 10 per cent between 1919–1939 and peaked at 25 per cent during the worst of the Great Depression, Australia quickly built and realised an extraordinary productive capacity as it armed and organised itself to fight in World War II. 'No financial or other obstacles have been allowed to prevent the need for extra production being satisfied to the limit of our resources,' the paper explained; 'it has shown up the wastes of unemployment in pre-war years, and it has taught us valuable lessons which we can apply to the problems of peace-time.'

Economists such as Ross Gittins refer to the period subsequent to the *White Paper* policy as a 'Golden Age'. When wages fairly remunerated labour, and incomes were spread more evenly throughout the economy, more people had greater purchasing power, and stronger internal markets were created for goods and services to be sold. Economics professor Chris Doucouliagos from Deakin University reported in 2017 that poverty does not, in fact, encourage people to 'strive more' and compete for wealth. Rather, economic inequality impedes access to education and training. Poverty—or the threat of it—removes the material means required for people to experiment and innovate in jobs or with businesses, or discourages them from taking that kind of financial risk. Insecure work conditions exacerbate this effect, as workers fight changes—like automation, or climate transition mechanisms—they perceive as threatening their income stream. Yet, 'Where workers' jobs are protected, for example with union membership,' writes Doucouliagos, 'there's often less resistance to innovation and technological change'. An excellent, immediate example of this is the nursing profession. Nurses are highly unionised, and that level of security and representation enables the union to provide ongoing training, so that nurses' careers develop along with the rapid pace of change and evolving technologies of medical science that are ongoing in their workplace.

Yet, by the time Malcolm Fraser came to power, neoliberals working for Treasury quietly redefined 'full employment' to mean a rate of just 95 per cent employment at any time. Unsurprisingly, it's a habit of neoliberal governments to make the experience of unemployment as punitive and humiliating as possible, to discourage people from risking it.

When public service jobs are outsourced or privatised, and when the alternative to a job on the corporate sector's terms becomes no job at all, competition in the labour market disappears, allowing wage and job conditions across the board to be driven down. Take the example of Australia's public-sector capital, Canberra. In 2017, there were 80,000 public servants out of 215,000 workers in total, but, thanks to a federal Coalition government employment 'cap' on the public service, no net new jobs were being created there; they were just replaced by 4100 part-time jobs. The Abbott–Turnbull government withheld wage increases from those who had held on to their public service jobs. The result? Fairfax reported figures from the Australian Bureau of Statistics confirming that wages for tens of thousands of Canberra workers had fallen 'dramatically short of the cost-of-living increases in the past 12 months'.

It is perhaps no coincidence that the Australian 'think-tanks' that advocate most passionately for 'cutting red tape', for 'small government' and privatisation, were founded by—and continue to be funded by—some of Australia's largest private employers. GJ Coles, the founder of the Coles supermarket chain, was the inaugural chair of the IPA.

The ideological objection to 'red tape' and 'regulation' only applies to their own enterprises, of course. When it comes to working people's organisations and right to take industrial action, they advocate as much red tape as possible, and have cheered on the imposition of some of the most unnecessary, resource-sapping, illogical over-regulation anyone could dream up. The Registered Organisations Commission (ROC) was imposed on unions after the Coalition won the 2016 election; its sole purpose is to police and regulate union activity. It was the ROC that directed the multiple raids on offices of the Australian Workers' Union (AWU) in 2017, the pretext of which was locating decades-old minutes that authorised a donation to the lobby group GetUp!. There was quite a media scrum when I arrived at the front of the offices of the AWU with its National Secretary, Daniel Walton. Just who tipped off the media to what amounted to a shocking misuse of government power is still under Federal Police investigation. The government raiding union offices in a democratic country is, of itself appalling, but consider this: at precisely the same time, Australia's self-regulating and poorly supervised banks were engaging in over 300 000 criminal activities, which the Royal Commission into Misconduct in the Banking, Superannuation and Financial Services Industry has since exposed. I note there has been no televising of raids on bank HQs.

The greater, darker, unforeseen consequences of privatisation are its corrupting effect on social fairness and opportunity more broadly. Corporations that acquire state assets depend on the election of governments with policies that will feed their business, rather than diminish it. It is in the interest of corporations that are paid to supply sub-contracted services to government projects, for example, to lobby hard against political parties mooting a return to better-paid, more secure, direct employment models. Privatised power companies that profit from a fossil-fuel-generated energy supply are obviously resistant to politicians promising to build and operate the infrastructure of renewable energy. The owners of a private bus company, or a pay-per-use toll road, do not want the government to build you a local train station.

A powerful incentive to corruption, hard and soft, exists in the dynamics of these economic and political relationships. Big corporations have a direct interest in politics and the political system; their political donations reward those who promise them favourable conditions, and neither the community benefit nor the national interest comes into it. One stark comparison is in the effects of privatised prisons: initiatives to reduce crime, reform sentencing or explore alternative justice models may be in the best interests of society, but they are fought bitterly by private prison operators.

When I was in South Australia in 2018, where the Liberal government had announced plans to privatise the Adelaide Remand Centre, it reminded me of a horrific situation that unfolded in America a few years ago. A Pennsylvania juvenile court judge earned a reputation for being 'tough on crime', sentencing kids as young as ten to stints in youth prison for offences as minor as stealing a jar of nutmeg or posting mock web pages about school teaching staff. In 2011, the judge was found guilty of felony corruption; *Forbes* reported that he'd taken $1 million in kickbacks from the private prison company that had bought the county's youth detention facility, and wished to keep it nice and full.

This is just one example of a systemic problem. There's now a worldwide industry of companies that offer rewards to political actors—politicians, lobbyists, think-tanks, activists—who show greater loyalty to maximising private corporate profits than they do to principles of equality, let alone the public good. It's parasitic capitalism, and it's the economic model that the opponents of fairness prefer.

Contributions in the *Australian Financial Review* have included declarations on this theme. 'It makes no sense to lock in anti-quated 19th-century notions of class warfare where unionism empowers the weak against the strong', wrote institutional economics professor Sinclair Davidson in 2018. 'This will simply benefit entrenched interests and disadvantage the young and entrepreneurial.' It's a variation on a theme that is repeated incessantly. 'In an unhampered, free-market economy', opined the IPA's Julie Novak for the *ABC News* website in 2014, 'the distribution of income is wholly determined by the interplay of mutually beneficial market trans-actions between sellers and buyers'.

A boss earning seventy-eight times as much as an average worker? *Mutually beneficial.*

Forty-four per cent of Australians in insecure work? *Mutually beneficial.* Five to eight per cent of Australians kept out of work, with the dole below the poverty line? *Mutually beneficial.* Tax cuts to a corporation at the expense of keeping the local school open? It's all 'mutually beneficial' … *apart from* the bit where nothing was 'mutual' about how these decisions got made, and that the benefits go to one side—and it's not the workers.

The culmination of these conditions of unfairness, exploitation and inequality is sending Australians back to the scene of that railway station in Clermont. The union workers are waiting for their cheap replacements to roll in on the train, but it's a trap—the coppers are there to break the strike, arrest the leaders, and do the pastoralists' bidding.

You can't heal broken bones with a bandaid. Little changes do not transform frameworks that are fundamentally unfair. The last few decades have enabled a record shift of money and power to a very few, but the remedy for inequality is what it has always been: collective action through the organised movement of working people. The trade union movement is the equalising, opposite force against the greed of the wealthy and privileged.

This is the reason why the wealthy and privileged are so relentless in their campaign to crush unionism.

Over the last thirty years, our movement has found itself on the back foot so often because neoliberalism as an energetic, activist project, has been on the front foot.

And its proponents have found ways to persuade just enough of the public to side with them. There have been intense propaganda campaigns to attempt to discredit unions and unionism in peoples' minds. Almost every day in some part of the conservative media there will be rantings aimed at smearing unions. It seems that generating anti-union media stories is a KPI for the Coalition government. They all make for a great show and come to nothing. Ex-rugby league player, now CFMEU official, John Lomax was arrested on a blackmail charge in 2015, and in 2018 got a payout from the Federal Police for 'wrongful arrest, false imprisonment and malicious prosecution after the charge was later withdrawn', as reported in the *Sydney Morning*

Herald. On a bigger scale, there was the Royal Commission into Trade Union Governance and Corruption that then Prime Minister Tony Abbott initiated. It took two years and cost $80 million, and had its own dedicated police force, and its actions involved tapping union leaders' phones, trawling through decades of union records, and raids on union offices. All of this uncovered one official and one bookkeeper guilty of misconduct.

Negative portrayals of what unions are and what we stand for saturate right-wing commentary. There are three preferred forms of attack: a numbing repetition of neoliberal insistences about economics that have been proved to be untrue; demonising stereotypes of unionists as dimwitted, peasant Godzillas; and paternalistic, very patronising, character assassination. In 2018, Janet Albrechtsen from *The Australian* wrote:

> … I have to admit I have a slight girl-crush on McManus. Of course, our politics couldn't be more different. Her cravings for more collectivism, more centralised power in the hands of union leaders are abhorrent to anyone who reveres individual freedom and understands that unemployment falls when the economy grows.

Then she said, even more bizarrely, McManus 'is just not a believer in growing the national pie'.

Oh, and Federal Minister Peter Dutton referred to me as the 'maniac' leading the ACTU. A case of projection?

The rhetoric is incessant, with the Murdoch press, big business and the Coalition not taking their feet off the pedal. They are desperate to prevent working people realising that campaigning for fairness alongside their workmates is the solution to low pay and insecure work. They'd prefer people maintain faith that trickle-down economics will one day (one day!) deliver pay rises; or that they find someone, other than their employer, and a system stacked in the boss's favour, is handily to blame.

A section of the community does buy the story the right spreads that it's 'immigrants', 'refugees', 'African gangs', 'single parents', 'dole bludgers', or some other scapegoat, who are to blame for economic and social problems. The cause of insecure work, unemployment, unfair taxation, weak pensions and low wage growth isn't any group of migrants. It isn't a religion. It isn't single parents. It isn't an unemployed person. It is a system of laws designed and implemented by a small group of people, to maintain their economic privileges ahead of everyone else's.

The likes of One Nation leader Pauline Hanson supply seductively easy, false solutions: 'stop immigration', 'ban Islam', 'reclaim Australia', 'get back in control'. But banning Muslims, Catholics, Baptists or any other group, or stopping immigration overnight, would not end insecure work or low wage growth, because of the people who make the laws that have allowed jobs to be casualised and wages to be kept low.

You don't fix unfairness with more unfairness; you don't get a fair go by denying one to someone else. You get a fair go by organising; by standing alongside everyone who's in the same situation and insisting on rules that ensure fairness.

My generation of unionists, in our forties and younger, grew up seeing a combination of anti-union laws, legal restrictions on union organising, and propaganda campaigns working to reduce union membership in Australia to 15 per cent. We experienced its slide, just as we experienced neo-liberalism hitting our shores. We learned the lessons of the 1980s and 1990s. Like those from the bitter Mudginberri abattoir dispute of 1983–85, where a picket by the Australasian Meat Industry Employees Union in the Northern Territory was smashed by a coordinated action of the National Farmers' Federation and the Meat and Allied Trades Federation of Australia, secretly assisted—as labour historian Bernie Brian revealed in an analysis of the dispute for the journal *Labour History*—by the Country Liberal Party. The union was sued by the employer for damages under the Trade Practices Act, and it was the first modern victory for a model of anti-union campaigning that fought its battles in the courts using cashed-up law firms—and its lead lawyer was Peter Costello. It was the same Peter Costello who represented the company Dollar Sweets, also in 1985, in an action that saw the trade union representing confectionary workers in a small Melbourne factory have to pay common law damages to their employer for losses suffered through a boycott—another

Australian first, and a legal precedent that we live with today.

Peter Costello, of course, went on to become Federal Treasurer in the same Coalition government that assisted Patrick Stevedores in locking out the Maritime Union from Australia's docks in the waterside dispute of 1998.

As a young organiser, I was one of many of today's union leaders who joined the pickets at ports across our country. I remember the shock of waking up one morning to hear that the wharfies had been locked out while we slept, and the feeling that spread across the union movement— and many other workplaces—that day: the instant unity that comes from outrage. An emergency rally was called, and all these people, from all these different unions that had never really associated, marched together down to the docks on the Hungry Mile in Sydney's Darling Harbour (now called Barangaroo). These were the days before emailing and using mobile phones were so widespread, and a group of us took it upon ourselves to get some clipboards and collect names, addresses and phone numbers, and organise the ongoing pickets through a phone tree.

We were down there every night. Sometimes there were arrests, and sometimes the police tried to drag us away, but the phone tree grew, and the crowds grew with it. The pickets stuck, trucks were turned back and, as the legal wrangling played out, the movement held its nerve. Then we won.

At the twenty-year anniversary of that dispute, unions and activists gathered for commemorations all around the country. People shared their different stories of the picket lines, in all the different places, celebrating not only what had happened at the docks but how it had made them feel. It was that experience of working class solidarity, of being brave and standing up, together, for a cause, and doing what's necessary to win against a government, boss or anyone else prepared to do what they can to destroy us. On the waterfront, the Prime Minister, John Howard, hoped for a victory over unionism itself, like that of his hero, Margaret Thatcher, when she broke the British miners' unions, but he was denied one. We'd taken on a well-resourced employer, a government, and the tactics of their whole ideological operation, and won.

It's that generation who's now come of age, and we know there are decades of damage to undo. There's collective recognition across our movement of two million people that we're not going to just absorb the hits from the neoliberals and their allies anymore. Unions are organising in workplaces, bringing people together and organising across the states, using face-to-face conversations, mobilisations, public debates and media old and new, to challenge the neoliberal consensus, and to promote the ideas that turn around inequality, by delivering greater job security and pay rises, and making the rich pay their fair share of tax.

We have learned a lot from the local neo-liberalism warriors, the likes of Nick Greiner and John Howard, through these years of attempts to demoralise, vilify and destroy us. You can only keep people pinned in a corner for so long until they start fighting back.

My generation of unionists has lived through it all, and learned lessons that have made us stronger, and more clear-headed about what the problem is that we face, who is to blame and what has to be done.

We will not be the generation to oversee the destruction of our movement; and, with it, the destruction of all the workplace rights, economic gains and progress towards fairness that our parents and our grandparents fought for and won. No way.

The article that appeared in *The Australian*—just after midnight—following my interview with Leigh Sales was titled 'ACTU Boss Sally McManus OK With Breaking "Unjust Laws"'. Ewin Hannan reported that I 'drew rebuke' from Malcolm Turnbull, then the Prime Minister, for my comments. 'Malcolm Turnbull accused the ACTU boss of seeking to be above the law,' the piece claimed, then quoted the Prime Minister himself. 'Militant unions have used bullying and standover tactics to trash the rule of law on worksites, and now one of Australia's most senior union bosses says the law should only apply when you agree with it', Turnbull said. He added: 'This flagrant disregard for the rule of law by unions is what has plagued Australian workplaces over

many decades. This is an explicit and out-
rageous admission. Labor's puppet masters
believe they are above the law. We do not con-
done breaking the law—not now, not ever.'

I wasn't even twenty-four hours into the
job and the PM was calling on me to resign.
As was a host of bosses.

Twitter blew up. My phone exploded.

There were calls coming from the commentariat for me to back down, as well as
predictions that I eventually would. Some
people even advised it.

Not a chance. The calls coming in from
other union leaders were 100 per cent sup-
portive. To us, what I'd said was unremarkable:
we believe that laws forbidding workers the
human right to withdraw their labour are
unjust. We always have.

And the difference between my union comrades' reaction and the reaction of the commentariat, the media and government, could not have been more stark.

The hysteria of right-wing commentators and the government—the sheer volume of their hypocrisy—was astounding. Here they were, each parading a view that suddenly demanded absolute fidelity to the law, when law-breaking by big business, and so many employers, is something they disregard. That's the ugly reality of labour relations in Australia: that laws are broken every day, not by working people or their unions but by employers. In recent years, unions have exposed epidemic levels of wage theft—a deliberate and illegal pattern of the underpaying of workers, which is a business model indulged in by, for example, franchisees of well-known retail brands, celebrity chefs and multinational corporations. Yet there's no moral condemnation from the right's favourite talking heads of the unlawfulness of this behaviour—no front-page articles, no obsessive pleas to affirm the 'rule of law'.

The unfairness could not be more apparent. Australian law punishes the strike action that demands fair wages, safe workplaces, job security and equal treatment for workers, and these strikes occur due to an employer's refusal to provide these things. When employers break the law and steal wages, it's in the interests of personal greed at the expense of working people.

It grates deeply on most Australians that there is one law that applies to rich elites and another, harsher standard applied to the rest of us. The deep contempt we have for their hypocrisy comes out on the occasions it is exposed. Witness the rage directed at former Liberal government Treasurer Joe Hockey in 2014, for enjoying a fat cigar after putting the finishing touches on a budget that devastated welfare payments; or the loathing towards CEOs demanding a cut to penalty rates while at a yacht regatta in 2017. This is because we know that affirming standards of injustice in the workplace establishes injustice as a principle in the broader community.

Suddenly, there I was, at the centre of a media storm of monumental hypocrisy whipped up by all those who had spent their lives trying to defeat us. People who'd remain unsatisfied if every one of my days began with me apologising for unionism's very existence.

The then Industrial Relations Minister, Michaelia Cash, denounced Australian unionism as having an 'atrocious record of lawlessness and militancy' and demanded that I be condemned.

Someone wise once advised me, 'When you're in the middle of a storm, stand still,'—so I did.

With the support of the rest of Australia's union leadership, the ACTU did not back down. I put out the following statement on 16 March 2017:

Australia has been built by working people who have had the courage to stand up to unfair and unjust rules and demand something better.

Every single Australian benefits from superannuation, Medicare, the weekend and the minimum wage—these were all won by our parents, grandparents and great-grandparents taking non-violent, so-called illegal industrial action.

Working people only take these measures when the issue is one of justice, like ensuring workers' safety on a worksite, a fair day's pay for a fair day's work or to uphold or improve the rights of working people.

Without the Australian trade union movement our country would look like the US where these rights are inadequate or do not exist.

There is rampant lawlessness in the workplaces of Australia and this is occurring in the form of chronic underpayment of workers, exploitation of visa workers, and workplace practices that put the safety and lives of people at risk ... This is what our Government should be focusing on.

And then—because work doesn't stop even when you're in the middle of a whirl-wind—I set off to speak, as scheduled, at a council meeting of the Teachers Federation.

It was on the way there that I realised I hadn't yet been exposed to what the broader union membership thought of what I'd said, or to what the general public thought. I was well aware of what the Murdoch press thought: there was still a massive media swell around me, including the printing of per-sonal attacks. This came from those intent on maintaining inequality, those who prosper through unfairness. The intensity of the media reaction showed that they wanted me to be afraid, to keep my head down. The government wanted to put a new ACTU Secretary back in her box. I had no intention of doing so.

Even so, things were a bit uncertain.

I walked into the Teachers Federation meeting … and found I was the subject of a standing ovation. From everyone. There were teachers union members in that room who would have been among the teachers striking in the Sydney Domain, back when I had my 'eureka' moment at the age of sixteen. Their response was the complete opposite of what I was getting from *The Australian*, the Prime Minister and the business lobby. The people in that room kept repeating: 'Thank god someone has finally said something like that.'

And from one end of the country to the other, from workplace to workplace, in all kinds of professions, union members still say that to me—over, and over, and over again.

That day, my speech to the Teachers Federation was improvised. I heard myself saying: 'I'm not afraid.'

I'm not afraid—not one little bit of them or what we face up to.

I just believe in the cause of fairness that the union movement has always believed in—and I will fight to realise the principle of equality for which we've always fought.

I believe our cause is just.

And I believe that if we pursue it honestly, even against the worst unfairness of the world, there's nothing—at all—for us to be afraid of.

I realise now that what I'd channelled was the instinct that awoke in me thirty years earlier, just a few kilometres from where I had been on the grass of the Domain. My words came from the passion of Tas Bull and Tom McDonald, and of all the elders who keep telling the stories of union struggle; and from the twenty years I have spent fighting the odds and alongside working people in my own union, the Australian Services Union. It came from the docks during the MUA dispute and from fighting WorkChoices. It came from decades of fighting neo-liberalism—the privatisations, the outsourcing, the demonising—and from all those years spent swimming against a mighty, mighty tide.

What the union elders try to teach us all is that it's the struggle itself that makes us stronger; and what the solidarity in that room of teachers reminded me, just as I first learned in 1988, is that unionism is both as powerful and as simple as people choosing to band together. It's why the enemies of fairness are many but why they can't defeat us—because when we have solidarity with each other, we have each other's strength.

Acknowledgements

I could not have written this without the work and assistance of Vanessa Badham, who poured her creativity, politics and time into it. Also thanks to Sally Heath for her suggestions and Linda Reed for her patience and assistance.

I'd like to thank the person who rarely gets publicly acknowledged for his long mentorship and support of my journey as a union leader, Michael Flinn. There is Tas Bull, Tom McDonald, Teresa Conrow and Cathy Bloch, who have all played important roles, but no one has been by my side and taught me as much as Michael.

Finally, I'd like to thank all the union members and delegates whom I have had the honour of working alongside. You have given me strength and every day you continue to give me energy.